When You Reach a Fork in the Road, Take It

When You Reach a

Fork in the Road, Take It

Lessons from the Business of Life

by
Bernard K. Bookman

Katie Folkman, Editor

Published by Interview You, LLC
Athens, Georgia
www.interviewyou.net

Copyright © 2009 by Bernard K. Bookman
All rights reserved.

Cover and text design
by The Adsmith
www.theadsmith.com

Interview conducted by Kimberly Torek

Photographs preceding each chapter are of
paintings by Bernard K. Bookman.

ISBN 0-9773365-7-3
Printed in the United States of America

To my loving wife, Brenda, and my daughters—Laurie, Karen, and Marnie—who say I don't talk about my past, so I thought I'd write about it.

CONTENTS

	Introduction	ix
1.	We Bookmans Did Our Own Thing	1
2.	A Montreal Childhood	5
3.	The War and Uncle Hymie	9
4.	School Days	15
5.	A Tough Grind and a Good Time at McGill	21
6.	Through the Gateway to the North	27
7.	Wouldn't It Be Nice to Have a Double Wedding?	35
8.	Newlyweds and Asbestos	39
9.	Business School and Babies	45
10.	Out of Academia, into Consulting	51
11.	Charlie, I've Got a Problem	55
12.	The Girls Grew Up in Florida	63
13.	Find a Need and Fill It!	75
14.	Looking Back	79
	INDEX	89

INTRODUCTION

Bernard Bookman's words leave the reader with an impression of profound conviction. Here, they proclaim, is a self-made man who has found the important things in life—close friends and family—but who wasn't afraid of pursuing a good opportunity along the way.

I have had the distinct privilege and pleasure of editing his spoken words from an interview transcript. For me, almost every response and every chapter yielded pleasant surprises—all the twists and turns that make up a full life. Retired and on the brink of relocating closer to family in Atlanta, Bernie Bookman's life thus far has indeed been full.

What impressed me most throughout the book was the way that Bookman defied convention at every step of the way—perceiving new opportunities at junctures where the others around him were falling into line and committing themselves to the expected path. Bookman, meanwhile, made a career out of the unexpected and refused to repeat the past. In fact, a fierce desire to avoid the shortcomings of his parents' generation gave him the courage and individualism to truly make a life of his own. It is that life, with all its twists, that makes up this book.

The only constants in Bernie Bookman's life as he tells it, in fact, have been family and adventure. Through Bookman's words and perspective, the reader meets Uncle Hymie; Bookman's wife, Brenda; and his three extraordinary daughters. His

story takes the reader from an ethnic neighborhood in Montreal to the north of Canada, and down to Florida and Hilton Head—just to name a few of the places Bookman has called home. Through it all, his words weave a narrative of hope, deep friendship, and the importance of being open minded in the modern world.

While showing tremendous adaptability, however, there is also a sense of moral responsibility—not necessarily to the system (as his chapters on drywall and immigration reveal), but to others and himself. With respect to those around him, Bookman shows the appealing, up-front attitude that has taken him so far, along with a good measure of vision and hard work.

As his book demonstrates, Bookman has put time and effort into his career, but also found a generous balance with an enjoyable lifestyle. His story maintains a sense of fun and enjoyment in every endeavor. From family man to business man, from engineer to artist and golfer and back, Bookman's story presages the current day and this era—one in which it seems more people exercise greater freedom regarding how to live their lives.

It is my most sincere wish that this book bring to life Bernie Bookman's ingenuity, spirit, and sense of honor—qualities definitely present in the original transcript and hopefully preserved to this final stage. Bookman is fond of quoting the saying, "When you reach a fork in the road, take it": interesting advice which I have endeavored to follow as I edited this book. I commend these words of wry wisdom to the reader as one key to the heart of this admirable and successful man.

Katie Folkman

CHAPTER ONE

We Bookmans Did Our Own Thing

My full name is Bernard Bookman. I was named after my father's father. The name is a translation of my Hebrew name, Ben Yuman, which means son of Yuman. I use a middle initial now, but it's not part of my legal name. It's the letter K, which I added to distinguish myself from another Bernard Bookman who lived in the same town where I lived. It was actually the bank manager who suggested I use a middle initial to keep us from getting mixed up when I went into business there. That, however, was much later in life, so I will begin at the beginning.

I was born in Montreal, Canada, in 1937 on the second of April.

My mother's name was Rose. My father's name was Abe. They used to call him Abie, but I never heard of any other name and I didn't have the opportunity to see his documentation. He was born in Montreal, and my mother was born in Winnipeg. Originally, however, my grandparents—both my grandparents on both sides—were Russian. I never knew my grandparents on my father's side; they died before I was born. But on my mother's side I knew both my grandmother and my grandfather.

My mother's maiden name was Kapustin, a very Russian name. Her parents immigrated to Canada just after the Russian

Revolution. I think it was probably easier to get into Canada than the United States at the time they immigrated. I know that a lot of people of that generation who immigrated to Canada were forced to do so through the United States; it was very common for European immigrants to go to New York first. But my mother's parents went straight to Montreal, stayed for a little while and then moved to Winnipeg, which is where my mother was born.

My grandfather had been an engineer in Russia but he couldn't practice engineering in Canada. So he went into the sewing-needle trade and had his own business that serviced sewing machines in Montreal. He ran that business for most of his life.

He died early on, when he was only in his sixties and I was seven or eight years old. It was in 1945, just two weeks before my uncle, his son, came back from the war. I remember the day when he passed away because it was my first memory of death, therefore traumatic in its own right. I was there, at home, when he had his heart attack. My grandmother, meanwhile, died much later. She was well into her late eighties when she died, so I had the chance to really know her when I was growing up.

From when I was born through my early childhood, my parents and grandparents didn't live that far away from each other. Even when I was very young, I used to go to my grandmother's house by myself and stay there often. I ended up spending a lot of time with her. I probably spent even more time at my grandmother's house then I did at home.

At home, I had two siblings, but our family was not very close-knit at any time—we just did our own thing. My brother, Harvey, is four years younger, and my sister, Eleanor, is eight years younger than I am. There was quite a gap in age between us all when we were growing up. At the time, I shared a room in my parents' house with my brother, but oftentimes I stayed at my grandmother's house. When I was at her house, I was really an only child. I even had my own room there. Ultimately, I felt more at home at my grandmother's house then I ever did at my parents'.

My father worked, like most men of his generation. He was a professional fashion designer, and he ran a fairly large clothing-manufacturing company. He designed ladies clothing—dresses and suits. He had the work ethic of the times, and he clocked a lot of hours at work. He also spent much of his time traveling to New York for his job. He would go down to New York for two or three days at a time and work with some fashion people there to bring back samples and things like that. I would drive out to the airport with him and back. At that time they were flying the old DC-3's; they were real clunker aircrafts. I never went with him, but I would watch the planes take off and land.

Meanwhile, like many women of her generation, my mother didn't work. Despite that, she had very little involvement in where we went or what we did, and my father had virtually no interest in our lives and activities.

Perhaps that's why I spent a lot of time with my grandmother; she was always there for me. It certainly wasn't because my grandmother was more lenient—she was a tough gal. She was very smart and very tough.

CHAPTER TWO

A Montreal Childhood

Where my family lived in Montreal when I was born was not your typical middle-class area. We lived in a mixed ethnic neighborhood. There were many French Canadians living there. There were also a lot of immigrants. I befriended kids of all different nationalities in our neighborhood. In fact, my parents were probably the only parents that had not immigrated from somewhere; every one of my friends' parents came from another country. It was interesting going over to those friends' houses and seeing how their families lived. A lot of them were from Russia, Poland, and Germany. We also had Italians, and we had Scandinavians. We had a little bit of everything around us.

I had a couple of really good friends. One lived in my apartment building, but he had to leave after his father died. That was my second experience of death; I was also there at the time. His father was a baker; he was carrying a heavy load of dough up to this third story apartment building when he collapsed and died of a heart attack. I supported my friend during that traumatic period. My other close friend lived just down the way, too. He stayed in Montreal and became a pretty renowned child psychiatrist.

We lived in an apartment, the third floor apartment of a three-story building. It was on Park Avenue very close to the mountains; it faces Mount Royal, the mountain in the middle of the city. When I was about three or four years old, we then moved down the same street probably five or six blocks and there we lived in a second-story apartment.

The apartment was in one of the older, small buildings—the kind that had stores and commercial space down below. Downstairs, on the street level of our building, there was a dentist's office in front and a grocery store over to the side.

Park Avenue itself was very wide; there were even streetcars running up and down it. It also had very wide sidewalks, which became our personal play space. My friends and I spent a lot of time playing on the sidewalks; we would roller-skate and play roller hockey and other games skating around.

I remember the snow; the snowfall was so heavy that there was almost always a snow pile between the sidewalk and the road, all winter long. We used to build tunnels in them. Then occasionally, about once a month or so, a plow would come and plow and take away this big pile, but there would always be more snow coming down. I would describe Montreal as a very snow-and-plow city. In the spring, we would see a city worker with a pickaxe coming down the sidewalk, using the tool to cut ice off the concrete. Some years, the ice that accumulated over the winter was six inches to a foot thick. It was not like New York or even Toronto, places where it gets cold and it snows sometimes, but the snow always melts off quickly. In Montreal, there was a lot of snow, and that snow stayed and the ice stayed, too. In the middle of winter, we would have spans of two or three weeks where it never reached above twenty-five degrees below zero. The wintertime was pretty severe, especially around the city.

During winter, however, we did have hockey to look forward to. That sport was the big thing. I played organized hockey myself from when I was six years old on. And I played well into my college years, too, but I was small for college teams. When I was young I was fast enough and good enough to keep up with everybody, but after everybody else outgrew me, I started getting pretty beaten up. After a while, I had to end my hockey career. When I was a child, we also went skiing frequently.

Overall, we played a lot of winter sports.

When the weather got warm, everything changed. We spent our summers in the Laurentian Mountains, about fifty miles north of Montreal. Our entire family, including my grandmother, would go together. My father couldn't stay the whole time, but he would come up when he could.

In the beginning, it started as two families renting a house together. Then, at one point in time, my father decided to build a cottage. After it was built, we would go up to our cottage and stay there for as long as possible. It then became a sort of family compound; it included two other homes, and we went there with two other families of relatives. While we were there, we would play, taking hikes and climbing mountains. The Laurention Mountains were a very pleasant place for us to be in the summer, both for the weather and the scenery.

That was also the norm at the time—families would get out of the city and spend their summers together. Part of the reason for the phenomenon was that when I was growing up, polio was a major factor in cities during the summertime. Going away in the hot months was then one way of escaping exposure to the disease. Ultimately, a lot of my schoolmates did contract polio, and often it had dire consequences. In fact, if that disease plagued people today it would be an utter crisis, but that's the way we lived. We retreated to the mountains.

CHAPTER THREE

The War and Uncle Hymie

I remember so much from around the time that the Second World War broke out. The war wasn't frightening for me on a personal level, but I do recall so much of it, perhaps because in your early years you latch on to the times that seem significant. The start of World War II was certainly one of those times of national significance. From the moment that the war broke out, and through the duration of the conflict, the atmosphere of the city was changed. During the war, there was a lot of energy generated from the consolidated support of the citizens of Canada. I imagine the attitude towards the war in the United States was similar at the time. The effort had the power to cross national boundaries. Also, within those countries, there was no infighting and no political mess; everything had to do with the war effort, the soldiers, and the things that you as a citizen had to do to support the war.

We all played a part, and everyone's lives were touched by the conflict during that time, even on a day-to-day basis. We had a rationing system in place for which we received these little coupons. In fact, everything was rationed. Altogether, we had meat coupons, food coupons, gas coupons, and coupons for miscellaneous things which we could only get a certain amount of each month. We also had to buy more coupons in order to purchase certain goods.

That time also brings back vivid memories of the blackouts we had in Montreal. As soon as the sirens went off, everybody had to shut off the lights and close down everything. We would close the blinds, stay indoors, and listen to the radio. At the time, we had this big radio with a magic eye [a special tube that glows to indicate when a station is properly tuned in]; I think it was a Philco, and everyone in the house would gather around it. Then we'd turn it on, tune in to the station, and listen to what was going on.

The war was a national issue. It was a personal one for us, too. In 1942 going on '43, it touched my mother's family. Her parents had five daughters and one son; the son was called into the service in 1943.

This was early on in the war, and my Uncle Hymie spent '43, '44, and into the fall of 1945 on the front. He spent time in both Italy and France, but he stayed in Italy for the majority of the conflict. He was wounded twice while he was in that country. One time, he received a bullet wound in the side. Another time, he was shot in one leg and subsequently jumped off a bridge, or maybe a cliff, and ended up in the hospital. We were never entirely sure of the details because Uncle Hymie was never very talkative about his war experience.

While he was in Europe, however, we always sent him packages. The act of putting together kits of packages to send him became so important because he had no communication with us most of the time. We'd send him some bits of food, some chocolates, cigarettes, and we would also add in some letters and a few personal items. We would send him those little containers constantly—especially after he was wounded. We all hoped for, and looked forward to, his return.

When he came back, he did so as a member of the Royal Military Regiment. After he came back, however, he was a very different person in many ways.

Because he lived at my grandmother's house before the war, I had grown up very close to him. He was a great person to look up to, and he acted as a sort of mentor to me. He was an excellent hockey player. He could have been a pro hockey player had he not gone to the war; he was that good. He was also a trumpet player before the war, and he played pretty well. He owned this beautiful trumpet, but when he came back he found that his mother had sold it while he was away. When he went away, he was also engaged to a gal, and they were ready to get married. Immediately after he came back, he found out that his girlfriend had left him. The broken engagement and his father's death overwhelmed him and, I think, changed his philosophy about life.

I remember going to the welcome-home ceremony; it was in a big field where all the returning soldiers came off the train. They all lined up, and there was a big parade and celebration. And he came off the field, and the first thing he asked was "Where's Pop?" He didn't know, and my mother didn't tell him, that his father had passed away. Instead my grandmother said he wasn't feeling well and that he had gone into the hospital. The family didn't tell him that his father was dead until after he got to the house. I was with him at the time in the car driving home, which I remember so vividly, along with how they told him.

He was so devastated by the news. I was, too—both for myself and on his behalf. After that, however, we became very close. Like I said, he was a changed person. He just became a fun loving, outgoing type. He took me everywhere. We used to play cribbage together a lot. As far as family is concerned, he was probably the closest family member that I had. He was a very tall, good-looking guy and he had a lot of girlfriends, but he just didn't want to have anything to do with getting married or being tied down after he came back. He went to work at an aircraft-manufacturing plant. Then, after he left that job, he became a taxi driver, and he owned his own cab.

He and my grandmother lived together from then on; he stayed at home and never married. Until my grandmother passed away, he was with her. He died soon after her. I can't even remember how old he was at the time, but we had stayed close through all those years. He was in his 60's or so, but I will always remember him coming back to Montreal as a war hero.

Now, with the war in Iraq, there's so much infighting. There's too much apathy. People here don't care about the conflict because they know they're safe. During the Second World War, we never felt safe. There were enemy subs off the coast of New York, and they were spotted all the time. The enemy was always close to us. That's why we heard the air raid sirens all the time. We didn't know whether we were being attacked or if we were safe. There was no communication.

Even though we were Jewish, we weren't aware of what was going on in Europe in the Jewish community; I didn't even know at the time and neither did my parents. I was more concerned about the war and my uncle coming back and that kind of thing; it never really had that religious bent on it for me.

CHAPTER FOUR
School Days

I was a good student and I liked school. I never really had to work hard; the academics came to me naturally and I was always ahead. In fact, I remember that during elementary school the teacher just put me in the back of the room and let me do all kinds of projects by myself while she taught the classes. I found the work easy all the way through high school, and I never really had problems. Socially, too, things were good. I ended up at the top of my class and as class president in my high school. I had a good time during those years.

I spoke French when I was in Montreal, of course; you learned French in English schools very early on. We learned French from first grade onwards, and we also used it on the street. So I spoke enough French to get by and then, of course, in my working life in Montreal I had to speak French often.

Math, however, was probably my favorite subject. From the beginning, I imagined I would grow up to be an engineer. I built a lot of models during the summer when I was a kid. During winter we had a lot of sports, but during the summer I remember sitting in the house building model airplanes. I built everything I could think of and made models constantly. I had a knack for it; I made a lot of good stuff. My room was always full of hanging model airplanes and model cars that I had built.

The first apartment, where I was born, and the second one were both on Park Avenue. Up to sixth grade, I attended Fairmount Elementary. It was a very long block, plus another two blocks away from our house. When I was very young, in my first years of elementary school, one of the neighbor kids who was a little older used to walk with me to school. I became independent, however, at a very young age.

When I think back, I can't believe the things I did at such a young age; I would never let my kids or my grandkids do what I did. I went everywhere by myself. I would get on a bicycle and go downtown or to visit friends and my cousins. My friends and I used to go to the movies. We had a movie theater called Canada downtown near where we had our first apartment, and we would buy the tickets for three feature films in a row for twenty-five cents. We'd sit through all three movies. Cowboy movies were our favorites; we were typical kids.

I also went back and forth to my grandmother's house by myself. My grandmother lived probably six or seven blocks away. I must have been only six years old when I started going back and forth by myself. I remember I did a lot of roller-skating during the summer, so I'd put my roller skates on and just take off towards her apartment.

When I was still in sixth grade, my parents decided to move away from the Park Avenue area, and we moved to what we then deemed the suburbs. There was nothing where we moved to, and it was quite far away from downtown Montreal. I had to switch schools. Even at the new school, I had to make this long trek with the streetcars and the busses down Iona Avenue. I had to walk about a mile just to get to a bus. I then took the bus three or four stops to get to a streetcar line and then hopped on the streetcar to go about two miles down to the junction where the school was, and finally I walked about a quarter of a mile to get to the school. When I started making that long commute by myself, I was only in sixth or seventh grade; I was about twelve years old. We had an hour and a half for lunch; many times I'd come home for lunch and then go back. That's back and forth four times a day.

I didn't have to lean on anybody. When I played hockey my father never went to see me play, ever. I played for years, even in organized hockey leagues. At the time, it didn't bother me, and I wasn't resentful about my parents' lack of interest in what I was doing because I did everything so independently. That included school, even from the very beginning. There was never a case where I had to come home and ask them to help me with my homework. In fact, my father only had about an eighth or ninth grade education. My mother had spent a few more years in school, but she had never graduated from high school or obtained a high school diploma. Her education was enough, however, to be a stenographer, secretary, and shorthand taker for a while before my parents got married. But she didn't work during the time that we were growing up. So I never really had anybody to direct me academically, and even at my grandmother's house, with my uncle and my grandfather, I never really asked for any help. It wasn't that they refused to help, I just never asked for it. I just expected that I had to do things on my own.

Then we moved to the suburbs, to a house on a street called Mackenzie Street. There were railroad tracks alongside Mackenzie Street, so from then on I was used to living in a place near train noises. And it was also somewhat near the airport, so we had planes flying over the home a lot. At times, we had to stop talking on the phone, covering the receiver and yelling "Hold on!" until the airplane passed. They would fly right over in those days, a practice which they don't allow anymore.

When we moved out to the suburbs I was already in high school, and my high school friends lived mainly down in the older section of town, which was where I had grown up. I did have some friends where we lived in the suburbs, but I didn't spend too much time there. Because I had such a long trip from where my parents lived, I was staying with my grandmother at the time. When I had to go home, I would hop on a bicycle and go from my grandmother's house to my house, back and forth. The route I had to take then was all busy streets filled with street cars and cars. I did it all by myself when I was twelve or thirteen, fourteen years old.

That was about the time of my bar mitzvah.

We were Jewish by heritage, of course, but we never went to the synagogue regularly. My father was a holiday religious person; he would only worship on the holy days. He wanted, however, for me to have the traditional bar mitzvah. So, before I turned thirteen, I was supposed to go through all the preparation and attend Hebrew school. Hebrew school for us was a very orthodox religious school. From the very beginning, I didn't enjoy it, but at first I would still finish school at three-thirty in the afternoon and go to Hebrew school from four to six o'clock every weekday and on Sunday mornings, too.

It was religious training by rote; nobody understood a thing. All we had to do was read Hebrew. I didn't understand the meaning of the words I was reading, but I had to read texts and I also had to memorize some songs. Truly, I didn't learn anything from the experience. There was no history. There was no teaching. There was nothing to inspire. There was just this: do what the teacher said and that was it, or you'd get your knuckles rapped.

So after a while, I started to play hooky a lot. In that time, I would go everywhere and anywhere. I would go to stores and just kill time there for an hour or two, simply to avoid going. My parents never found out a thing about it. Occasionally, the rabbis would say, "Well, he didn't show up," but I would always find some kind of excuse.

I went ahead and did my bar mitzvah, but that was really the end of my religious career. I had no use for the synagogue in a spiritual way; I had my own philosophy, and because the Hebrew school experience discouraged me, I couldn't be religious in that way.

Anyway, after the bar mitzvah, I was going into high school. In Canada, there weren't separate middle schools; you went up to seventh grade and then you went into high school. At that time, my parents and siblings moved to Westbury Avenue, near a new high school. It was, in fact, both an elementary and a high school. My brother and sister went to school there, but I had since moved out to my grandmother's house to live there while going to high school.

The high school that I went to was very close to where my first apartment was and near the mountain. My high school was Barron Byng High. It was one of the most prestigious high schools in Canada. It was in an area that was predominantly a Jewish neighborhood; therefore, a lot of my classmates were also Jewish. Many of them I would call high school buddies, but I wouldn't say that there were any close-friends relationships. It wasn't until I got into college and fraternity that I started to get into close friendships.

CHAPTER FIVE

A Tough Grind and a Good Time at McGill

I went to school at McGill University, in Montreal. It was very cosmopolitan, a very well-known university worldwide. It doesn't seem to hold the same prestige in the United States, but it's respected everywhere else in the world. They have a great medical school–a world-renowned medical school, in fact.

Despite any reputation, however, money was the only deciding factor in choosing a college for me. In Canada then, however, you didn't pay for tuition. College education was very subsidized; I think we students paid approximately two or three hundred dollars a year to go to college. Even so, I was

Bernie with his 1952 MG TD, Montreal 1957

Bernie and Laurie, Montreal 1965

Bernie and Brenda engaged! Montreal 1960

Bernie, Brenda, Karen, Marnie, and Laurie, South Florida 1971

able to afford that education only because of McGill's location in Montreal. There were no dorms, but my parents couldn't afford student living anyway. I just went to McGill; I didn't apply anywhere else. If you lived in Montreal, and you stayed in Montreal, a McGill education was the usual path that you followed when you went to school. Even so, at that time only about ten percent of my high school class went to college. It was not a time when everybody went to college. You had to earn your way, and you had to get good grades to get in. Most of my high school buddies just went into business with their families directly. In the end, only a handful of us from high school, maybe five or six students, ended up enrolled in college; we all went to McGill.

I technically lived at home, staying with my family. My friends and I, however, had a fraternity house on the campus, and I spent a lot of my time around there. The fraternity was a great organization. We reactivated a chapter that was on campus back in the '20s and '30s but had been inactive ever since. It was called Sigma Alpha Mu. We were so close, the seventeen of us that reactivated together, we were like family, and perhaps even closer than I had been with my immediate family. We spent a lot of time in the fraternity house, certainly more time there than at home, despite the fact that most of us were from Montreal and still lived at our parents' houses.

I liked college; I enjoyed my time and I did well. I didn't have any major problems, and I finished probably in the top ten percent. I remember, however, that it was also hard work.

Most of my buddies from the fraternity were not engineers. There were only three of us in the fraternity that were in the engineering program. The other, non-engineer brothers had a lot of leisure time on their hands. We, meanwhile, never had free time per se. It took five years to get an engineering degree from McGill. It was a long grind, five years of college and, then, for our final exams in the last year, we had seventeen final exams in two weeks. And a lot of them were open-book exams, which meant that it was not memory work. It was harder because you had to go through the stress of thinking through problems while you were sitting there taking your exams. It was a lot harder than trying to memorize a few things and do it by memory. It wasn't nearly as tough as business school, but that came later, and I thought college work was quite difficult at the time.

Anyway, we always had the fraternity to let off steam. We threw a lot of good parties. We all had a good time at those parties and just spending time together, too. We also had some solid, serious people in there, and the people that graduated with me from my fraternity all did very well in their lives. I keep in touch with some of them, but a lot of them ended up leaving Canada. A lot of them immigrated to California and a few other places. There were still a few left in Montreal, but they were successful there. Like I said, there were not too many people that went to college at that time. Those who did go to college had a good start. Now it doesn't matter. You graduate and it doesn't really mean that much.

CHAPTER SIX

Through the Gateway to the North

I probably leaned more towards my grandfather because he was an engineer and I ended up being an engineer. Maybe I went in that direction because of the background from my grandfather, although if so, it was subconscious because I didn't really plan it that way. In fact, when I went into the first year of college, I was signed up for architecture, which is a combination of engineering and art. But after the first year I saw that architects weren't making that much money unless you were really up there. So I switched to engineering, and I graduated as a mechanical industrial engineer.

The requirements of the college engineering curriculum, however, went beyond the academic experience. Besides class work, each engineering student had to have a certain amount of hours of practical experience in order to earn an engineering degree. Engineering students had to have engineering apprentice work as credit. As a result, a number of companies came in and gave engineering students apprentice jobs for the summer vacations, and our summers were long. We finished approximately at the end of April and didn't go back to school until the middle of September. We had quite a May, June, July, August, a good span of time to acquire some practical know-how.

I was hired on to a company called Hydro, Ontario Hydro; it was a huge, hydroelectric power company out of Ontario. They sent me up to their northeastern-region home base. The first year I was there the home base was in Timmins, Ontario, fifty miles south of James Bay, which is the southern tip of Hudson Bay. I was about 700 miles north of Toronto. It was almost unfathomably north. North Bay is considered the gateway to the wild north, and after North Bay, which is 250 miles north of Toronto, I had to go probably another 300 miles in order to reach Timmins.

The first time that I went up there I was seventeen years old. The only way to get up there was by train. I naturally got on a train in Montreal, and when the railroad employees gave me my ticket, they said, "Stay on the train and we'll get you up to Timmins." So I got on the train and remember it going quite a distance. I was in a sleeper car and eventually I went to sleep. Then, when I got up in the morning, the train wasn't moving.

I looked out the window and there was nothing. It was totally desolate, with one little shack sitting alone in my view. I got dressed and poked my head out the door to realize that I was sitting alone on a siding with only myself in a single car with no train. There was nothing else there. I was on a siding and that was it. No one told me anything about what to expect; I sat there and waited. I probably waited three hours, at least, and I had no idea what to do with myself. There was nobody in the shack, so I walked around. The landscape was similar to bush country. Even though it was the end of May, it was remarkably cold outside. There was still snow all around me. It was melting, but it was still snow. Three hours later, a slow moving old train comes in, backs up, picks up my car, and off we go.

There was nobody there to even ask about where we were going. There was nothing. I mean there was just the engine and while there may have been a couple of people in the other cars, I never even saw them.

The car was labeled the Ontario Northline Railroad, so I deduced that if it was called the Ontario Northline, it must be going north. This satisfied me enough that I was headed in the right direction, and I eventually ended up in Timmins.

Timmins was a gold-mining town, and at that time there were about ten thousand people living there. I was picked up at the station by an employee of the Ontario Hydro, and they took me to Timmins. They set me up in a home, where I lived for the summer. The owner of the home was a Catholic priest in town; Father Therieau was his name. That summer, I went to Catholic services with him solely because he was a very interesting character. He was also the only priest in the town, so there were a lot of people coming and going to our house all the time. It was still a great arrangement for me because he had a housekeeper and decent food. He used to make me sandwiches every day that I spent in Timmins and pack them in a lunch pail.

I ended up spending a lot of time away from Timmins, however, because we would travel all over that region for Ontario Hydro. Just south of Timmins was an airplane and seaplane base for the company. We used to have to fly from there to the sites to work on the dams. The water from North Bay travels north, not south, into Hudson Bay. All along that stretch in that period of time, Ontario Hydro had dam sites and hydro-electric plants, but there was no access to them. It was in a grid, but there were no roads or anything. So you had to fly in.

So we'd fly in for anywhere from two days to a week at a time and work at those locations. The planes we flew in were bush planes, the really small kind that could take off and land almost anywhere.

During the time I spent at Timmins, I had one really good friend with me. He was the son of a timber company owner. We used to fish, canoe, and hunt together. We ended up with long hours and even in the time off, we had to stay in Timmins—there was nowhere else to go from there—but we got good pay. We earned time and a half and double time and double time and a half in a lot of places. I was not earning a very high hourly salary, all things considered, but because of all the extra time we spent, I always left with a lot of money in total. I had enough money to stay in school, and that was how I paid my way through—by spending my last four summers working for Ontario Hydro.

I went to Timmins two summers and then they sent me to North Bay. In North Bay, the first year I stayed in a United minister's house. I went to Sunday services with him every week. He was quite an interesting guy. Looking back, I'm not sure why they placed me with religious leaders, but it seems to have been a trend.

The second summer in North Bay, however, I stayed with the editor of the North Bay newspaper and then spent some time in Cobalt, Ontario.

Cobalt is about halfway between North Bay and Timmins, approximately a hundred miles south of Timmins. It's part of the tri-town area, which is a big silver-mining location. The town itself, however, was surprisingly small. There might have been maybe two thousand people living there. If you ever saw the television program "Northern Exposure," with its footage of the corner store and a moose going down to it, that pretty much sums up a typical Cobalt scene. In fact, I used to watch that program just to see the background of it and remember my time in Cobalt; while the show wasn't filmed there, wherever it was filmed is almost the spitting image of it.

During the course of the engineering apprentice program, there were a number of other students that went up there and were given a very hard time, but I wasn't one of them. The local people would put everyone through a period of time in which they would make it very rough. If a student didn't take it with good humor and react the way they thought he should, he was going to have a pretty terrible time, and that was what happened to a number of the other students that went up there. I learned early on how to deal with those rough-and-tumble people. They were tough and rugged, but underneath, to use a little bit of a cliché, they had hearts of gold.

For example, when I was up in Timmins we would meet early in the morning before different crews would disperse, and three people would go to this place, two people would go that place, and so on. So the very first time I was up there, the foreman, one other guy, and I all got into a truck, and we went to a location. When we got out, they said, "Look, we got to build a road through this area," and they gave me an axe and told me, "Look, we're going to have to bring some more equipment out here. You start and you'll have to cut the path through. Here's an axe. Just start cutting through the brush."

I spent that whole day by myself in the bush. By the end, my hands were so sore and blistered from cutting through with the axe. The next day when I came into the shack, they were roaring. All of them were laughing their heads off. The day after that, they came out with bull dozers and big equipment and with the push of a button just cut a swath through the area I had been working on. It was all that kind of big joke, the good-natured hazing, that you had to take back then to be part of the community; and let me tell you, they looked after me following that. If I had a sniffle, even, their wives were there to take care of me. That was the kind of people they were.

It was a very hard life for them, with a very different lifestyle. For instance, there was no way to get good meat at a reasonable price up there. They would have had to have it shipped from a butcher in Toronto. So they would go out and kill a moose instead. Each family was allowed to kill one moose a year. Just one moose, however, would give them enough meat for the whole year. That was the way they did things out there.

When I was up there, we would fish and hunt together. From those expeditions, we would then eat what we had caught. I know living off the land that way wasn't easy, and the winter season was really tough when the temperature would drop down to fifty below zero.

While I was never up there in the heart of winter, the last year I was there up in Timmins, when I got there in May, there was a snowstorm, and when I left on the last day of August there was another snowstorm. As we used to joke, "Summer was on a Thursday last year." That extremely northern location also had its advantages, especially in the summertime when I was there. At night, we could play baseball at eleven o'clock, and it was still light. Then, at two thirty in the morning the sun would rise and it would get light again.

There were the northern lights, too, a gorgeous spectacle in a sky that was pure black at night. It was breathtakingly beautiful, but I had no desire to stay for a winter.

In the end, I enjoyed that summer work. The experience on the whole was just fascinating. At first, they gave me some pretty tough jobs and a lot of grunt work; for example, they would make me crawl into the big, huge turbines and clean out the inside of all the worms and the grubs. They also made me paint the super structures on top of dams; to do so I would have to climb up to dizzying heights, strap in for support, and paint.

It wasn't what I had imagined it would be for the first year or so. After a while, however, they put me in the machine shops and then I could do more of the engineering aspect of the work. So it became interesting work to me. But, after my fourth summer, I had already graduated. They asked me to return, but I just didn't want to get stuck with a career up there, which would be pretty bleak. So I declined and went to work for a large company, Northern Electric, which was the predecessor to Nortel, a manufacturer of telephone-communications equipment. It was in Montreal, which was a bonus. The conditions, however, were not ideal. I had to work in a big, eight-story building alongside two thousand other engineers. It was a manufacturing facility. I ended up spending about two years with them.

Anyway, I still have great memories of the summers in the north, and they got me through school.

CHAPTER SEVEN

Wouldn't It Be Nice to Have a Double Wedding?

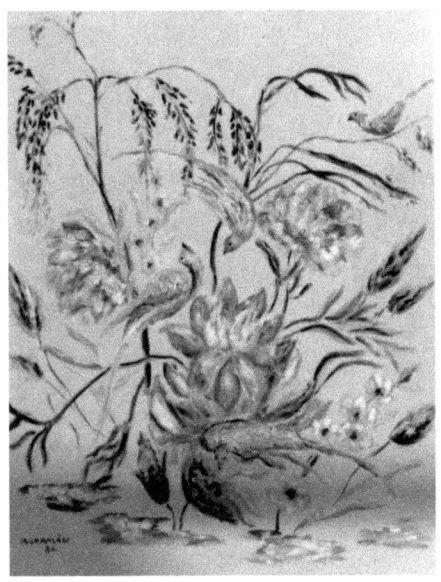

My wife, Brenda, never went north with me on those summer trips. Even though I met her while we were both at McGill, I met her after my last trip, when I was in my final year of school.

Before Brenda, I had about a girlfriend a year in college. In the wintertime, I had to make sure that I went out with a woman who had hockey tickets. Then, I met Brenda.

We met through the fraternity parties—it was a "scene."

Generally, we would have beer and invite friends over to the house. How we actually first got to know each other is a funny story. My wife's a twin, an identical twin, but I didn't know that at the time I met her. I knew her twin, Linda, first. Then, when we were at a party one time, Brenda was sitting there on the side, so I went over and I talked to her as if I knew her, not realizing that she was the other twin. She probably thought I was nuts at first, but after we got to talking, we hit it off right away and exactly a year and four days after I met her, we got married. We ended up having a double wedding because Linda was already engaged to a guy I knew from another fraternity. She had been engaged for quite a few years, so they had already set a wedding date.

This is how it happened.

Brenda would say, "So when are we getting married?"

I'd say, "Soon, babe, soon."

So we figured that it was easy enough to do, and finally there was a discussion between her parents and us, one in which they suggested this: "Wouldn't it be nice to have a double wedding?"

The wedding was huge. My father-in-law was a very prominent dental surgeon in Montreal, the head of the Jewish General Hospital and of the dental school. He was a very well-known man around town. Because of all my father-in-law's connections, we had well over five hundred people at the wedding. We even had people that crashed the wedding; people that were not invited just kept showing up. It was just jammed, and everything was so elaborate.

That night, I wondered what I had gotten myself into—there were times I was dancing with my wife and not knowing whether I was dancing with my wife or my sister-in-law because they were absolutely identical that night, even to me: they had the same dresses, they had the same tone of voice. They also wore the same makeup, which sort of blocked out most everything that differentiated them. I had to be very careful with what I was saying because I didn't know who I was talking to. That was one spectacular wedding.

We went to Nassau and Jamaica for our honeymoon afterwards and had a great time. It was my first time really out of the country. That is, if you consider Timmins as still in the country; that place was about as "out of the country" as you can imagine. Of course, I came down to the United States often, but I don't consider that out of the country. So my first time out of Canada was with Brenda, on our honeymoon. It was a great beginning to our new life.

It was 1961; I was twenty-three and Brenda was twenty-one. While I was immersed in physics and engineering, she was an English and history double major. She earned a master's degree and became a teacher when she graduated from McGill.

CHAPTER EIGHT

Newlyweds and Asbestos

After we were married, Brenda and I got an apartment in a neighborhood that was still in the suburbs at that time, although it was starting to be built up quite a bit, even at that point. We moved into a small apartment building that was about halfway between her parents' house and where my parents lived.

It was all new, but at the same time the transition to being married to Brenda was an easy one. Before we got married, in fact, from the time we first met, Brenda and I had a lot in common. We became best friends before anything because we liked outdoor activities a lot. We used to go skiing together. We hiked a lot and took walks together, too. Once you're friends, the relationship gets away from this artificial, dating mode; it becomes more natural. We shared a love of the outdoors and even after we were married, we did a lot of camping, hiking, and traveling together. I always thought it was important to be friends with her, too, and share adventures, so that's the way it worked out.

At Nortel, I befriended three men who were also working for Nortel: Paul Brown, Sam Barnes, and John Anderson. We had a lot in common: they had all just gotten married and they also joined Northern Electric at the same time. Anyway, even if the fact that we all worked together at Nortel brought us together at the beginning of our friendship, we also spent a lot of time together away from the company. The friendship even included our wives. In fact, Brenda became close with their wives almost immediately. Each of the other couples had their own interests, but interests that were coincident with ours, like hiking and camping, so we did a lot together. The four of us on one hand and our wives on the other were, in my opinion, the closest that you could ever imagine people to be. We were all the same age, and we also started to have children at the same time. We still send Christmas cards back and forth with them, after all these years.

All three of them live in the Toronto area now. Two of them stayed with Nortel for all those years and eventually retired from the company.

John Anderson, meanwhile, became CEO of another large company in the same kind of work. I have to tell you a funny story about John, bearing in mind that I met John as soon as he came off the boat from Scotland with his wife and we had been so close through my time at Nortel, when we were young men. Anyway, years after we were working together, Brenda and I were up in Toronto at another friend's wedding. I hadn't seen John in about twelve years. We were corresponding, keeping in touch, but I hadn't actually seen him. Anyway, I called him up to make arrangements to go see him. So I go to his house in Toronto, knock on the door, it opens, and there's John standing there. It was like going back in time; he hadn't aged at all; he didn't even have one wrinkle or a single grey hair, and this was decades later. In fact, he even looked a little younger. It just floored me; I was speechless. In the end, it turned out to be his son, John, but at first, I had no idea. That story also gets at the sense of generational continuity between our families, even when we were no longer in Montreal together.

I didn't leave Canada until the beginning of 1970, but we did spend some time away from Montreal. Right after a couple years at Northern Electric, I decided to change jobs. I was doing very well through this large corporate structure: I was getting the best raises and the best promotions, but I couldn't stand the pace of this bureaucratic, large corporation. It was driving me nuts. So I went to another large corporation; why I don't know.

I went to work for a company called Johns Manville, and they sent me to their asbestos mine in Asbestos, Quebec. It was a really small town, with the largest open-pit mine in the world. In addition to the open-pit mine, they also had an underground mine and a mill there. They hired me on as the industrial engineer for their mill operation. That was the first time that I took Brenda away from Montreal. She had never lived anywhere else. She was apprehensive, I'd say, but mostly it was an exciting opportunity. It wasn't a problem between us; it was just, "Here's an adventure, and we're going away."

Brenda was very close to her family, especially her sister at that time. Later on not as much, but at that time they were extremely close as twins. Despite all the ties, we went out on our own; we went on a trek. We rented a house in Asbestos, Quebec.

Brenda took on a job as an English and history teacher in a high school. She claims to this day that she had students in her classroom that were older than she was. But, despite the students' ages, at that time and in that setting you didn't have any disciplinary problems in high school. It was a really good high school atmosphere, and she really enjoyed it.

But we didn't stay in Asbestos too long, almost less than a year. I had a better job offer to come back with the father of a friend, in fact a fraternity brother; his company was Eagle Toys, and Eagle Toys was the largest toy manufacturer in Canada. He was also the single inventor of the push-pull hockey game. He invented that and a few other things. So he asked me to come back and work for him in the design department. Accepting the position was probably a mistake because he was not an easy guy to work for, even as an engineer.

It was in my capacity as a mechanical engineer that I came to the toy company. I was both a mechanical and industrial engineer at the time. The two are very different kinds of work— for example, in my industrial engineering job I did time studies in asbestos. I was trying to work on simplifying the problem of loading and unloading bags of asbestos along with other projects like that: the kinds that involved trucking, transportation, and conveyer belts. Mechanical engineering, meanwhile, is all design. The toy company needed that kind of engineer; even in toys you have to design things like plastic molds.

Regardless, that job moved us back to Montreal. I stayed with them for half a year or so, and then I left them and I went to work for ITT wire and cable. They had a plant in Montreal, and ITT is, of course, a large company, but they had bought a company called Royal Electric. Royal Electric, while it was owned by ITT, was also a self-sustaining manufacturing company, mainly in wire, cord sets, and stuff like that. Within three months of working for them, I became the plant manager for Royal Electric. I was only about twenty-seven years old, which was very young for that kind of established position. I stayed with them in that role for a couple of years, and it was a good job. I was even earning good money, but then I began to think about where this engineering could take me. At that time, I was only four years out of school, but I was already seeing huge changes from what I had studied. The field was advancing so fast that skills became obsolete very quickly.

CHAPTER NINE

Business School and Babies

Eventually, I decided that it would be better if I went back to school in business. I had a long discussion with the president of Royal Electric and ITT in which I told him that I was going back into a business program. He told me, "Yeah, that might be a good idea, but you're very welcome to come back when you finish this two-year training program." He treated me so well during the summer and between semesters at business school. Whenever I had a break, he welcomed me back to the company and paid me full salary during the time I was there. Because of his generosity, I was able to pay my way through school. He really made it possible, especially because we were starting a family at that time, so money was tight.

Laurie, our eldest daughter, was born three years after we got married. When we had Laurie, it was a real big thing. We were such proud parents!

Even with the new baby to take care of, Brenda completely supported my decision to return to school. She is a great believer in education. Her father was very well educated, her mother was well educated, and she was well educated; school was so important to her upbringing. With her agreement, I made the choice and off we went. We went to London, Ontario, so I could attend the University of Western Ontario. The university there was truly the Harvard of Canadian schools, as far as business was concerned. In fact, it was so patterned on Harvard's business school methods that we used Harvard textbooks and we had professors from Harvard visiting our classes all the time. It was very prestigious and also hard to get into. We only had a hundred people in our class.

Brenda and I spent two years in London, Ontario. We had a great time there and became very close friends with some people there. Like a lot of young married couples, we had a townhouse like so many other students who were living there. There were children and new families around us; it became a social network. That's how you really get to know a lot of people: through the wives and the children of your fellow students. I remember we had a few parties while we were in business school, but we did a lot of work. It was really a grind, much harder than getting an undergraduate degree.

The subject came to me naturally, even if I had to work more than before. I was again in the top five percent of my class and became the president of my class as well. In that sense of accomplishment, I enjoyed the business school experience.

Meanwhile, Brenda didn't work because she was taking care of our new baby, Laurie. As our firstborn, she was so special to us, and she required all our attention and care. All that I remember of first meeting her as a newborn was a big block of black hair, but that was before they allowed men in the delivery room. From Laurie on, we planned our family without any trouble. After Laurie, we waited three years to have Karen, and then almost two years later we had Marnie. It was very well-spaced, and so we became a family of three daughters.

We were a family of females, that is, except me. Overall, I felt completely outnumbered in the house as a male. Later, after we moved to the United States, it became even more comical when even my dog and horse were female. That, however, was much later. All three children were born in Canada. We didn't move to the United States until my youngest was one year old.

From the very beginning, this family was totally different from the one I had grown up in. This new family of mine encompassed both my children and my in-laws. One of the key changes in my life at this point was that I became very close to my father-in-law. He and I became fishing buddies; we would go away on weekend trips together to fish. On those trips especially, we discussed everything. Although he was a dentist, he was very interested in what I was doing professionally as well as personally, and we just sat and talked a lot. He was a great guy; I would describe him as a truly beloved man, well looked upon and well liked by everyone in his community. My relationship with my father-in-law was completely different from the one I had with my father.

Brenda's family wasn't wealthy, but they were well off compared to my parents, who were always lower-middle class. My father never had any money, but he never had a lack of a job. He worked for one company all of his life, and he was secure that way but never really had money for anything non-essential, nor was he able to really enjoy it. He became a cautionary tale to me, not someone to emulate professionally. So I entered into a different world of opportunity when I got married. I even liked my mother-in-law's cooking; my mother burned everything. My whole way of life changed.

For instance, in my family at home when I was young everyone was very modest. I mean nobody walked around without clothes, and emotionally everything was kept very close to the vest. At first, seeing Brenda with her family, compared to my childhood household, was like walking into a nudist colony. There was something very free about it, a spirit which carried over into our house later—as soon as we went home in Florida, everybody ran around without clothes on. It was all very different to me; I would describe it as very open—my wife is a very open person. She tells it like it is. She would get into trouble a lot that way with the kids, but you know there's no hiding anything with her.

In terms of religious influence, Brenda's family was almost the same as mine; they were not strict religious people. My father-in-law, however, was very pro-Israel. He gave a lot of money to Israel through bonds and investments like that. He was also very active in the Jewish community fund-raising campaigns and other philanthropic efforts. He was not in any way zealously religious; however, he did have a conservative, community perspective on Judaism.

We never really had any huge family gatherings of the kind that would involve both my parents and Brenda's. Of course, any family gatherings that my parents participated in were mostly through the effort of Brenda's parents. We would get along with both sides of the family, but I don't remember having any get-togethers or parties or anything like that.

CHAPTER TEN

Out of Academia, into Consulting

I became an assistant to the manufacturing industrial professor, marking papers and doing some of his research. He was really trying to talk me into staying in school after I got my MBA. He even offered some pretty good scholarship money for me to stay and go on for a Ph.D. The offer definitely tempted me because I felt an affinity for the school. Additionally, I knew that I enjoyed the teaching aspect because I had done some of it in the professor's absence; I was an assistant to him my last year. I saw, however, that there really wasn't any big money in academia, and at the time I was making the decision, job offers started to come in from potential employers. At one point I had eleven offers, real job offers—it seemed then that the offers were all over the place.

Then I had another professor who was a partner in a consulting firm that was owned by Coopers & Lybrand. Coopers & Lybrand was one of the big, worldwide accounting firms. The professor started to talk to me; he had to pick two people that he wanted to hire. At that time, in 1966, no accounting firms and very few businesses had employees with MBAs. This professor picked two people that he wanted to have join them with job offers as management consultants to start their consulting divisions. So he picked me out of Western, and he picked another guy, Ken Taylor, who was a family friend of the professor's and was graduating out of Toronto. So, he talked both of us into joining and that's how I met Ken Taylor. He comes in later in the story, but Ken and I signed on as the first MBAs in Canada to join Coopers & Lybrand's consulting division.

They didn't really know what to do with us. It was the early stages of computers, but they had a lot of business and mergers and acquisitions. In other words, they were doing a lot of large-scale turnarounds. In the end, it worked out that we would agree to take on whatever problems the accountants couldn't handle for the company. Ken and I spent a couple of years together working for Coopers & Lybrand and traveling. We did one huge, general waterworks utilities merger, which was about an 800 million dollar merger, and we did all the work with one corporation as their backup accountants. We did computer installations, which were a huge investment at that time; a basic accounting installation would cost the firm a minimum of a hundred thousand dollars. Now you can buy one computer to do it all. At the time, however, we did all that work.

We didn't really know anything about computers back then. In engineering we didn't even have computers. In fact, at the time I graduated with the engineering degree, we were still using slide rules and little handheld calculators. Computers just came in when I was in business school; we had one of the first computers there in 1964. It was just a big building with a bunch of wires; it was then that the first IBM 360's had just come in. Our computer training was in FORTRAN, which is the original language of the basic programming—back when companies didn't have any technological infrastructure.

We didn't have any idea that computers would take off in the direction they did. No idea whatsoever. In fact, we were saying that there was no future in programming. We truly believed that the programmers were there for the early stages of computers, but after a while the computers were going to program themselves, so there would be no need for the programmers. I was thinking at that time that programming was not a good career choice. You know, things change.

Through our jobs, Ken and I traveled everywhere. We did most of our work in the United States, but we also did some work in England because Coopers & Lybrand was a British firm originally. We did some training in England. I liked the country, but it takes a little of the enjoyment out of it when you go to work in a place. It was also hard on Brenda when I was traveling so much; she stayed home with the kids, and I left on Monday morning and came back on Friday night. Later on, however, my wife spent some time with her sister over there for several months because of her sister's husband's work in England, and Laurie was over there, too, for a while. We spent a lot of good, career-focused time with that group.

In the meantime, ITT was trying to get me to go back

after my MBA. They offered me a job, but I had to go to their headquarters in Pawtucket, Rhode Island, and so I went down to Pawtucket and took one look around, and I said, "I don't think so." I just had such a negative gut reaction to the place. So, I declined the job offer.

It was a hard decision for me because the company had been so good to me. They helped me through school and supported my higher-education goals. When I talked with the president of the company in Pawtucket, Rhode Island, he said, "Look, if you ever decide to come back, the door's always open for you," which was reassuring to have as a backup because I didn't know what I was getting into in consulting. It was rather new. Anyway, I had some plans up my sleeve and that was how I got to Florida.

CHAPTER ELEVEN

Charlie, I've Got a Problem

At the end of 1969, we moved to the United States. We first moved to Hollywood, a town in south Florida, just below Fort Lauderdale. They had a group of Canadian businessmen, a group of ten businessmen who bought a big chunk of land from the Arvida Corporation. It was just west of Fort Lauderdale. It was raw land, and they had to put together some kind of financial plan to see where it would go, to talk to the architects and engineers and basically put it all together from nothing. I went down for a three-month consulting job. At that time, I left Brenda at home. This was the fall of '69, and Marnie was just born. She was born in '68.

When I finally brought Brenda and the girls down to Florida,

I had to leave them alone in a rented place in Hollywood while I worked from morning until night. But I had them come down, and we rented that place and I took on this job, and then they asked me to stay and run it for them. I made a plan; I had an attitude of "Well, let's put it together." So I spent a couple of years with them and we invested about seven million dollars putting together this project and all the infrastructure it required; we built roads, water, sewer plants, and drainage districts. That's how I got into real estate and the development business; before I came to the United States, I didn't know anything about development.

At the time, I had no reservations about leaving Canada, because so many people like us were leaving the country. The separatist movement was very strong; there was a lot of flack about French versus English. Brenda wasn't too happy about the school system because they were forcing French out of the English education. It became a very messy situation, and eventually a lot of people were getting out of Canada. My brother-in-law was a neurosurgeon then, and he joined the United States Army and went to Vietnam for two years just so that he could move to the United States and legally practice medicine. So off he went, and they moved to Houston and we went to Florida, and a lot of our friends also left for places like California. It wasn't a far-fetched idea to move to Florida.

We stayed in touch with my wife's parents, however, and we

visited each other. They came to us mostly because we had the kids, which made it difficult to travel. Occasionally, we went back, but not very often; it was so easy for them to come down here. They spent time in Florida every year; they would have come down anyway. We also had Canadian people staying with us that we never even knew. We had family that visited us and slept on the floor that I had never seen in my life.

With the kids, we had this house in Hollywood, paid 39,000 dollars for it. It was a three-bedroom, one-bath house, 1,400 square feet. We started out in the United States with all five of us living in this tiny space. So we moved in, and we enrolled the kids in school. A couple of years after we moved, we put them into the Nova school system, which is a gifted program there, a top-rated school as opposed to all the other schools around, which were not very good. So we were lucky to do that, but Brenda had as much to do with it as luck, because she pushed her way through, and she pretty much ran the schools after a while.

One day, however, we got a knock on the door, and we opened it to find officers from the Department of Immigration on our doorstep. "Can we see your papers?" So we show them the passports and all that stuff. One of them then asked me where I was working and other questions. I replied that I was working for a Canadian company. Because I was employed by a Canadian company, I was being paid in Canada, but working down here. They politely said, "Well, you're not really supposed to do that. You should have a regular visa to be able to work and apply through normal channels. You'll have to come down to the office and talk to us."

I made an appointment to go down to their office in the next couple of days. We were all set up in Florida at that point, with our own house and the kids in school. At the immigration office, we had a brief discussion and to make a long story short, they said, "Well, you're going to have to go back to Canada. And you will have to come in through normal channels, get a proper visa and then come back."

"Well, how do we do this? We've got kids in school and all that stuff you know. And I'm getting paid in Canada. I'm not taking money out of your pocket. I'm getting paid up there." They maintained that they couldn't do that. So anyway, it just so happened that in the community I was building up, we had already built a golf course and other amenities, and I had golfing friends who were in the immigration service down in Miami. I also knew someone on the border because of my consulting work in the United States. (Whenever we crossed the border with that job, we had to go through this charade of saying that we were going into the United States, but not really working in the country, and every week we went through the same act. And it became almost laughable to the point where we became friends with the immigration people because we were going down there so often.)

So, at this point, with immigration breathing down my neck, I said, "I've got to do something." I called up one of my golf friends and I got the name of one of the chief guys in

Montreal and his name was Charlie. I called the number and said, "Charlie, I've got a problem."

So he told me, "Look, you come up here and I'll have you speak to a few people and see what we can do." So off we go to Canada. We have an appointment with Charlie in his office. We go visit him.

"Look," he says, "I talked to immigration. It so happens that your wife may be eligible for U.S. citizenship." Apparently, Brenda's grandmother immigrated first to New York. Her mother was then born in New York, and when she was a baby they immigrated to Canada. "So," he said, "when you [looking at Brenda] were born the law was in place where if you had a parent born in the United States you could be eligible for United States citizenship." "But," he says, "you [looking at me] and the kids can't be eligible."

When I talked to the immigration people, they said they would grant me and the kids a visa but they could not grant my wife a visa because she might be eligible for U.S. citizenship so they couldn't let her in. So Charlie said, "Look, I talked to someone in the state department, and I set up an appointment for you. You go to the state department and they'll grant you parole to let everyone through, but immigration will not recognize it." So off we go to the state department and get our piece of paper, and then he said, "This is what you have to do: you have to drive down to the border by car. You have to meet this person at the border, and he will process your parole visa and let you through down there."

So off we go. We go to Canada. We go through all this stuff. We come back and we end up back in parole; they still don't know what to do after processing. Well, very shortly after, I get a call from Charlie. I said, "Hey, what's going on?"

He said, "You'll never believe this, but I've just been transferred to head of the immigration service in the Miami airport."

So he comes down, becomes a good golfing buddy and, through him, all the immigration guys and I get together socially. I get them free golf because I just built my own golf course. We're all buddy-buddy, hanging out and playing golf together. I process my papers immediately; no problem at all because of my new friends. The odd part was that Brenda was never recognized by immigration as being a citizen of the United States, but the state department gave her a passport. Meanwhile, Linda, her twin sister, tried to process papers, and they would not grant her U.S. citizenship. She had to have a green card.

So she's sitting with a green card for all those years while my wife was a U.S. citizen unrecognized by immigration. That's the story. It shows you how important it is to have friends in the right places; if I hadn't, I would still be sitting in immigration today.

I didn't fully became a U.S. citizen until we moved to Hilton

Head, South Carolina, about twenty years later. I couldn't get close to the Florida immigration system, especially the Miami immigration office after the Cubans started coming in, and then right after that, the Mariolitos came in. It was so jammed up you couldn't even get inside that place. So I never even bothered with going down there. Then when I moved to Hilton Head, I found out that Charleston had an immigration office, so off I went to Charleston and processed my papers, and I went through the swearing-in ceremony and everything else.

After all these years, Karen and Marnie just recently got their citizenship, but Laurie is still a Canadian citizen. She has this loyalty; I don't know where it comes from. But it's a lot easier to travel Europe or other places with a Canadian passport than it is with an American one. As soon as they see you have a Canadian passport, attitudes change. I don't know why, but for some reason in a lot of places they don't like Americans.

CHAPTER TWELVE

The Girls Grew Up in Florida

The girls grew up in Florida. They went to good schools. All of them did very well, and they were involved in extracurricular activities—Laurie, especially, was very active in swimming. I had to take her to swimming practice at six o'clock every morning. The other two were very active in band. They were all-state for years. I mean they got draped with medals in all-state competition in music. And they were all placed pretty well in college because they had good enough grades to go anywhere they wanted to. Their education worked out very well.

We were a good parenting team. My wife was the disciplinarian, no question about it. I was the softie; I melted. It was almost a slight problem in our family because my wife said I wasn't strong enough with them. But you know, with little girls, you can't tell them no, so what do you do? You melt. I have the same problem with my grandkids. As a matter of fact my little grandchild, the youngest one, a girl, comes over and kisses me on the cheek and says, "Papa's melting. Papa's melting." She's only four years old now. But you know I always found it hard to discipline little girls that were so cute.

As a family, we did a lot of camping. We didn't really travel

Bernie and Brenda at Marnie's wedding, Atlanta, GA

Marnie and Bernie's father/daughter dan

Bernie riding Bijou, the family's Polish Arabian

The Bike Ride Across Georgia, Bernie, Brenda, Dale, and Karen

Bernie's barbershop quartet, Hilton Head, SC 1999

Bernie and Brenda at the Hilton Head annual show

Bernie's fishing trip in Northern Quebec, 1972

Brenda and Bernie skiing in the Laurentians, Quebec 1960

that much because we were in Florida; we spent a lot of time at the beach or weekends away. It's hard to really travel with young kids anyway and, additionally, we had a dog and a horse.

We spent about a year and a half or so in Hollywood, and then one of my friends was developing some land in Davie. His family had owned a big orange grove out there for generations, and he took that orange grove and split it up into one-and-a-quarter acre lots. After he subdivided it, another friend was a builder, so we built our home out there in the orange grove. At one time, we had seventy-five orange trees on our property: it was beautiful.

It was in the cards that the people who had originally intended to develop the Arvida property weren't the group to foot the bill for that development because it would take a lot of money and a lot of time and they were all, at that time, in their sixties and seventies. All they wanted to do was build a golf course and a few homes around it, but we had a potential project with ten-thousand homes built on an enormous piece of property. So I talked them into selling it. They got what they put into it, which was okay, and we sold it.

Then I was ready to leave, but then I spoke with my partner, who was in charge of my account of that real estate project. He was also a golfing buddy of mine, and he was a partner of Leventhal Horthwath, which was the tenth largest accounting firm in the U.S. with offices all across the country and headquarters in Miami. He said, "Look, we want to set up a consulting division. We need someone, and you've got a lot of experience with that. Why don't you come work with us; why don't you stay here?"

I was ready to go back to Canada because I didn't know what to do without a job, and I had to get paid in the United States and not in Canada. This was only two years after the immigration-status problem, so I figured I'm not going to be able to stay anyway. He talked me into coming down and joining them, however, and I set up their consulting division. I became a manager; you can't become a partner in an accounting firm unless you're a CPA. Because I was an engineer and MBA, I was sort of stymied; I became a manager but I couldn't become a partner. They paid me good money, however, and I did a lot of work and I traveled across the United States setting up their divisions in consulting.

So I spent a couple of years working for them. The job involved a lot of travel—I went to Turkey, France, and Germany, among many other places. Anyway, after I joined that firm, I got involved with some other clients of that firm in community-development projects. So I finished what I had to do for setting up those divisions, and then I was really self-employed because I had project after project after project in development. One such project was Seagram's. Ken Taylor, the guy who joined me working for Coopers & Lybrand at the beginning of my consultant career, ended up with the real estate arm of Seagram's, and he wanted to have someone in Florida to head up their real estate operations. The company owned a lot of land there. They wanted to bring it all into development. So he got in touch with me, and then I joined the Seagram's group. Here's a roundabout story, but that's how I got my horse.

One of the clients was up in Palm Beach County where we were doing development work; he owned a farm and he had horses. He had some beautiful animals there; among them was a two-year-old Polish-Arabian mare that he had sort of as an extra. He told me, "You know what? The kids would love to have a horse," and he gave me this gorgeous Polish-Arabian. They're very expensive animals, and Polish-Arabians are a fancy breed. So we brought her home, and we kept her on our property. All the kids learned to ride.

We had absolutely no real knowledge about horses, only trail rides, but that didn't count as experience with horses. Anyway, we loved our mare and took good care of her. Her name was Bijou. She was a light gray. All the kids learned how to ride western-style, and they also learned how to ride English style.

So this place where we built this house was in Davie, and Davie was horse country. It had a population of ten-thousand people and ten-thousand horses. Even the McDonald's in downtown Davie had a hitching post. Kids, especially girls, would get on their horses after school and all you could see were girls on horseback all through the town every day. Young girls and horses seem to have an affinity for each other. Anyway, that was just typical of Davie, and the kids had a ball.

I earned good money, and I began to realize in very short order that in Florida lifestyle was very important in a career, that if you didn't enjoy the way you went about your day, it wasn't worthwhile. So, at three o'clock in the afternoon everyday, I was out playing golf. We also had a lot of good friends down in Florida, and Brenda was in the women's association there. She was really active in a lot of things. We had a good time together.

Every one of the girls worked. Laurie worked at Subway and the other two kids worked at Wendy's; I had to pick them up at night smelling like stinky meat. The food-service smell permeated everything. It was enjoyable for them, however. They weren't working for money. They were just working for the experience.

During high school, Laurie also decided she wanted to work with animals. She went to a vet, and she offered her help for nothing to work with him. She did that for quite a few years. In the end, she learned an awful lot about veterinary stuff. That's how she knows a lot about animals, including turtles.

When the girls dated, they brought home the weirdest, geeky guys. Twice I literally threw people out of the house. I had been very active in Montreal. I had skied. I had played hockey and kept fit, too. When I got to Florida I did a lot of running and track and all that stuff, but I still needed some exercise. One day I was passing Hollywood and there was a karate studio there, so I went in and I stayed in karate for, oh, ten years or so, and I got a black belt in *kosho ryu kempo*. Later on I earned a master's level in tai chi. So I was pretty adept in convincing people, and I guess I was an imposing figure to the guys that wanted to date my daughters.

While the girls brought home a lot of weird people, they also had a lot of good friends, too, especially in their band. The band kids were super. We went to Europe with the band five times as chaperones, all in the course of the girls' high school years. Laurie made one trip; Karen made four trips and Marnie five trips. They went all over Europe, even behind the Iron Curtain when it still existed, going to Czechoslovakia and Hungary before the wall came down. They played in many top places: in the Vienna opera house and in London. They also had joint concerts with kids over there. It was just phenomenal. They were really good, and they played in a great band.

I would like to think of myself as the complete opposite of my parents in terms of parenting style. Brenda and I were there for our children all the time. We were at every competition. If they were part of the band at the football game, we went to the football game. We were involved with their swimming. We even went to dance recitals. We cared about everything. No matter what, we supported them, and we still do. When they have anything going on, we're there.

When the girls went off to college, it would have been hard emotionally, but by that point we had an RV. We got that RV in '87, and we put 110,000 miles on that thing, traveling around following our daughters. We had one girl at Rensselaer Polytechnic Institute (RPI) and we had one girl at Brandeis and we had one girl at Emory. So we traveled; it was our solution to missing them, and the RV was great for what we needed. It made it easier for us to go on our own timetable, and we ended up sleeping in the RV in parking lots at the universities. It was fun because we were alone, just us and the dog, Poochie. We had already given the horse away to a camp for underprivileged children. It was a tough decision, but we had to do it because we were traveling a lot and a horse needs more taking care of than a dog, let me tell you; a horse is totally dependent on you for everything.

Anyway, we visited the girls. We brought them to school with the RV; we were able to bring their luggage and all that stuff. We picked them up, we delivered them, and we brought them back and forth for holidays in that RV. It was just grand. But after a while, this was in '89, we were still living in Florida and we had this great big house and all the land to take care of. We decided we were going to have to sell the house. So we sold that house. We were almost thinking of going back to Canada at that time. But then I got a call from Ken Taylor again. He kept on coming back. He said, "I'm not with Seagram's anymore. I'm doing some development work at Hilton Head." He told me, "I've got a property management group division, but I don't really want to do property management. I want to just do development work."

In the meantime, I had already done probably five developments all the way from Miami up to Palm Beach. So he said, "I've got a couple of things that I'm doing in Florida, building retirement centers. I've got one in Hypoluxo (which is in the Palm Beach area) and one in Sarasota." He said, "If you could look at those things, go and visit and see what you think you can do with them, and then perhaps come up to Hilton Head and see if there's anything here for you."

So I went over and saw these projects. I said, "Yeah, I can take care of them." So I took care of those projects for a while. I got them through zoning and had them all planned out and everything else. Then, after that, Ken Taylor said, "Why don't you come up and see about this property management thing in Hilton Head?"

Off I went to Hilton Head, and I took a look at what he had there. It was really a small operation. It had a couple of employees, and he had at that time maybe about a thousand timeshare weeks that he had developed. A thousand timeshare weeks divided by fifty is only twenty units that he put up. So I said, "Well, I don't know if there's much money in it and everything, you know, but I can give it a try."

Brenda and I wanted to move anyway, so we said let's go up and we'll rent a place at Hilton Head and spend some time and see if we can put something together. It was Brenda and I and two other people. We started putting together the property management phase; we set up the company and separated ourselves from the development arm. In ten years, I had ten thousand weeks under management. I had a hundred permanent employees. For ten years in Hilton Head we really put together a good company that gave us a nice lifestyle. We built a beautiful home there, right on the Harbortown golf course. I had a good staff, and being my own boss, I was able to play golf, and we both got very involved with the community. Brenda was the president of the herb society, and she got involved with the women's club. We had a lot of friends; there was a good group of people within the Hilton Head. Once you're involved in one thing, it's almost as if there's a list, a list of activities people will add you to as soon as they find out that you're available.

So, we kept busy. It was a small town. At that time it was 8,000 permanent residents. Aside from the resort population, and there truly were a lot of visitors, the permanent population of Hilton Head made up a small town. Now it's about 25,000 people, but it was about 8,000 then. So we had a great lifestyle with some great people.

CHAPTER THIRTEEN

Find a Need and Fill It!

I'm going to tell you just one fast story to fill in my work experience and illustrate the way things happened. While I was in Florida and I was doing development work—this was in the early '70's—there was a huge increase in building activity in the United States. It was the first time that development went over two million units a year in new buildings across the states, and this resulted in shortages, one of which was drywall. We absolutely could not get drywall. Well, this was in the middle of the winter season when there was a lot of building activity and a lot of demand for housing, and these huge corporations, like General Development and Levitt Corporation, were building multi-unit developments. It was just massive construction going on, and very severe shortages of drywall developed.

So I was talking to one of my friends who came from a very wealthy family, and he was really a playboy of some kind, always looking for something interesting to do. He said, "Why can't we get some drywall to supply some of these guys?"

"You know," I said, "drywall's not easy. You've got to carry it, you've got to transport it, you've got to have trucks." And I'm sitting there thinking, soon after, a few days later, I was mulling around in my mind, thinking: "In Canada it's the middle of the winter, and they don't have any construction activity." It virtually comes to a halt. And certainly there's drywall up there. So I go to the Montreal yellow pages and I see a bunch of drywall suppliers, the biggest of which was a company that sold building supplies. So I called them up, and I spoke with the owner. I said, "Look. You know there's a shortage of drywall down here. Is there any way of us getting some?"

"Well, maybe," he said. "My biggest supplier is U.S. Gypsum, and I just happen to have three trucks that I use to haul vegetables from Florida to Montreal during this time of the year and I dead-head back. But you're not allowed to transport dry products in vegetable trucks. (They call them reefers, refrigerated trucks.) You're not allowed to do that." "But," he said, "I've got a lot of drivers who know their way through that could get across, get through the weigh stations and all that stuff. But I have to figure out a way of how to get the drywall on and off the truck because usually drywall is delivered by flatbed where you take your fork lifts and just lift them off, but with reefers you have to get inside, and you got to pull them out."

So it took a couple of days, but he got back to me. He said, "I've got a way." (This guy was a French Canadian with a French accent.) "I've got a way of doing that." So he sent us a truck on the side with some long forks. In three months, we were hauling ten to twelve trucks a day. We were getting reefer drivers; we went to bars in Florida that nobody in his right mind would ever walk into to find them. My partner and I would walk into these bars and everything would be quiet as soon as we walked through the door. And we'd walk in and everything would be quiet and we'd say, "Who owns these trucks outside?" We talked to the drivers. Well a normal load from Montreal to Florida would be about $1,500 by flatbed. We were getting reefers at $500 apiece to pick up because they were also deadheading back. In three months, we made $50,000 in cash over a kitchen table.

Brenda and I will always remember that one day I walked and the kids were all sitting around watching television. My pockets were full of hundred dollar bills. Suddenly I pulled out the bills and threw them up in the air. There were hundred dollar bills all over the place. We were selling to Levitt and General Development. We were supplying some of the biggest projects in the country.

Anyway, three months later, the drywall situation started to ease off a bit. By the way, during the shortage, we had been up-charging these boards, selling them for a much higher price than their normal distributors would have charged them, but they needed the board. So they were paying almost double the price. They were paying us in cash, no checks, just cash. It was amazing. When it eased off a bit, too, these companies said, "Why don't you stay? Stay with us; you can supply us this way. Why don't you call up the companies and you stay in business and we'll give you our business."

So I called up my company in Montreal and I said, "Hey

these guys want to stay in business. Can you keep supplying?"

He said, "I'll come down and talk to you." So he came down and we set up a company to sell drywall in two locations: Hollywood and Hialeah. Using his credit line, we got credit from USG and Gold Bond building products, which were the two best. We were shipping twenty-five flatbed trucks a day for these people for two years.

It just so happened that after two years the markets dropped. The distributors, the companies themselves, USG and Gold Bond, decided that they were going to get out because the prices started to flatten. They were going to get rid of their distributor way of operating and go direct to these large companies, and they knocked out all the distributors and virtually put us out of business after our three-and-a-half year run. That's just one example, however, from the story of my business life.

CHAPTER FOURTEEN
Looking Back

I've been retired for ten years now. I love it. It took me about a week to get the office out of my system. I like my golf, and my leisure, so I joined the club here. I'm having a great time playing golf a couple of times a week. There are 200 guys here that golf, all seniors, and we really have a good time together. I stayed in Hilton Head immediately after I retired, but we are spending quite a bit of time in Atlanta where our children and grandchildren live. I've got a lot of equity built up in that house; it's my whole retirement there.

We decided to move because my wife wants to be with

the kids and the grandchildren, especially now that my third daughter has decided to move down here from Boston and the other two of them are already living here. Once we move, the whole family will be together.

I never thought in terms of family because I never really knew what family was until I got married. Brenda's relatives showed me what family could be, and I learned a lot from them. In the end, I even got along better with my mother-in-law than my wife did. When my mother-in-law got ill, she was in her eighties, early eighties, and she had lived in an apartment all by herself since my father-in-law passed away. It was quite a long time of being alone, so when she got sick, we decided to bring her down to Hilton Head. She probably had the best two years of her life in Hilton Head, and I had a good time with her, too. We went out; we drank together. She was my drinking buddy; we had dinners and we had a good time. She stayed lively until the last couple of months before she passed away in her bed at home at Hilton Head. I was there holding her hand during that time. We feel very good about bringing her down and having her spend that time with us. It's something that we saw as a duty, but for us it was an enjoyable one. Our relationship with other family members, however, became much more estranged.

My wife and her sister haven't spoken for probably eight to ten years. They had a falling out. I still find it hard to think of them as twins not speaking to each other. Her brother, meanwhile, has a very close relationship with our family.

It's the same with my siblings. My brother lives in Florida

and my sister lives in Ontario, a little town near Toronto. I only speak with my sister occasionally. She comes down and visits once every three or four years, and that's about it. I haven't seen my brother in forty years. My brother and I had a falling out decades ago when he got married. His bride had a younger brother of ten or eleven years old, and she talked my brother into making the kid his best man instead of me. I didn't really care for that, so we had a falling out. The situation just exaggerated from that point, and we never made amends.

Our family is our immediate family: us, the three girls, and the grandchildren. Other than that, we really don't have any other family close to us.

Laurie has already earned three degrees. She went to Brandeis and graduated with a psychology degree. Then she earned an MBA and went on to get a master's degree in accounting. Karen lives in Boston; she works for Dow Chemical. She's a Dow Chemical superstar. She's an RPI engineering graduate in bio-medical engineering. My youngest daughter, Marnie, is an Emory graduate, a PysD in neuro-psychology. She's an assistant professor at Emory and does consulting work for various people, including jury trials.

I remember being so proud when both Karen and Marnie won the Westinghouse award scholarship. Both of them won it for medical projects. They both went to the summer science programs at the University of Georgia in Athens each year, which led to the award. Karen won it one year, and a year later, Marnie won. Westinghouse only has a hundred students a year in the whole United States that they give this award to through the Westinghouse science program. To have two sisters, my two daughters, win it back-to-back was phenomenal. It was unprecedented—there were presentation ceremonies by Westinghouse executives especially for them. The whole experience was characteristic of my daughters and their achievements.

I have four grandkids, two girls and two boys. Becca, Benjamin, and Mollie Nadolne are Marnie's children, and Adrian Winkler is Karen's. My wife loves to be involved with them. I can take them for a day. The noise, however—I can't take the noise. They're good kids, but you can't keep kids quiet or down, and I just like my quiet time. But I do play golf. So I get away, and that's okay. My wife, meanwhile, spends a lot of time running around and shopping with the girls. She spent all day yesterday with Laurie, and that's fine with me; it gives me some peace and quiet.

So I am going to be seventy in April, but as long as I don't look in the mirror, I don't feel seventy. Fortunately, I also have my health. I had a stent put in my heart about seven years ago without really a major problem. I just had a little shortness of breath, and they found I had an artery partially blocked, so they put the stent in, and ever since then it's been fine. My greatest accomplishment has been surviving, or living on borrowed time. My father died at sixty-one, so I've got nine years on him.

The males in my family had a history of heart problems. My father had his first heart attack at fifty-nine, and he died at sixty-one. My mother died much later. She was well into her late eighties, just like my grandmother. She was senile, and she ended up in a retirement home in Canada and just didn't know what was going on. If my father had had the medical care of today, however, he would have lived a lot longer. But he never went to a doctor. He didn't take care of himself. My father worked for one company most of his life, and one of the reasons I think he had a heart attack is that the company went under. One of the owners was a brother-in-law, but my father ended up with no pension, no money, and no job at fifty-nine years old, without any idea of where he was going to get his next dollar. He had put everything into that business. He was there six days a week; he got up at six o'clock in the morning and came home at seven o'clock at night, but he got nothing out of it in the end. Watching him, I promised myself I would never put myself in that kind of position. I never got to the point where I hated what I was doing, either. A lot of people are in that situation; they hate their jobs because they never looked outside them because they were lured in by the sense of security. I promised myself I'd never get into that rut, something I've seen a lot of people do. When I worked at Northern Electric, my first job, one of the reasons I left is I saw 8,000 people everyday at five o'clock rush to the cloakroom and hurry down the stairs to get out, hating every minute of every day, and working for twenty and thirty years like that, day in and day out. I decided that that would never work for me.

It's a great accomplishment that I am pretty well respected in both the business community and in my personal friendships. I seem to somehow get along with people, although I don't think I was that soft in business, but I had a lot of respect for and from my employees and I seem to have struck a good balance. Perhaps I could have done more with my career, but you can always say that. I think I got the best of my career path in that I've never been bored and neither has Brenda.

The move to Florida was also unanticipated; I never thought that I'd end up in Florida or Hilton Head. People I knew when I was young are still surprised when they first find out that I am not in Montreal anymore, forty years later. I tell them that I am living on Hilton Head Island, in this paradise. They wonder; "well, how did he get there?"

If I had to give anyone advice it would be to take a risk. You can't do anything without taking a risk. Sometimes that is really hard to do because people like to be in their complacent comfort zones. I believe there is a disadvantage to having too much privilege at the start of your life; I've seen people without the advantage of having gone to college, with their backs up against the wall, be very successful because of it, not in spite of it. When you have to do something you do it. You can get very comfortable sitting in a corporate office and getting a salary paycheck for thirty years—hating every minute of it, but not having the guts to get up and do something about it.

Every time I got into a situation where I thought I might be too complacent, I remember my father's situation. I used to think, "Pop, you can't do that; you've got to move on." It was tough sometimes to just take the leap and do something new. I didn't know how it was going to turn out. I could have fallen flat on my face at any time, not knowing whether I would have a job the next day or have a successful project, whatever it was. There was always a risk. When you take the risk you can't really worry about where you are going to get the next buck, and that could be tough sometimes.

Looking back on my life, I can't picture it in terms of expectations or dreams. I never really imagined anything because at the time that I started to look for a job as a career, the general attitude of workers at that time and the general attitude of employers was this: you join a company, you stay there for life and you retire and get a gold watch. A few people who I knew early on did that, but most didn't. As the majority of us discovered, your first career is not necessarily your last career. I changed directions so many different times that I can't technically call myself an engineer anymore. Fortunately, I went to business school, so at least I could handle financing and other jobs like that. Some of the work, however, was beyond anything I could have anticipated; for example, I got into management consulting, developed golf course real estate developments, brought drywall down from Canada and started up a building supply company, and owned a property-management company in Hilton Head. Those opportunities just came along, and I grasped them.

This is how I lived out my personal motto. As I have said since I was a kid and as my daughters still remember me saying, "When you reach a fork in the road, take it." It doesn't matter which way you go, but make a decision and do something. Don't just sit there and look at the road. That's the story of my entire career. I never really looked for a job. There was always something going on for me to be involved with. I never left a job for money, but it was never entirely about the money; I focused on the experience, the possibilities.

It's worked out fine for the last seventy years.

INDEX

A

Anderson, John   39-41

Arvida Corporation   55, 62, 66

asbestos   41-42

Asbestos, Quebec   39, 41-42

Atlanta, Georgia   ix, 64, 79

B

bar mitzvah   18-20

Barnes, Sam   39

Barron Byng High School (Montreal)   20

Bijou   64, 68

Bookman, Abe (Abie)   1
- Bernard K. (Bernie)   ix-xi, 1, 22-23, 64-65
- Brenda   v, ix, 23, 35-37, 39-42, 45-49, 53, 55-57, 59-60, 64-65, 69, 70, 72-73, 77, 80, 84
- Eleanor   3
- Harvey   3
- Karen (Winkler)   v, 23, 47, 61, 65, 70, 81-82
- Laurie   v, 22-23, 45-47, 53, 61, 63, 69-70, 81-82
- Marnie (Nadolne)   v, 23, 47, 55, 61, 64, 70, 81-82
- Rose Kapustin   1

Brandeis University   70, 77, 81
Brown, Paul   39
business school   25, 45-46, 52, 83

C

Canada   x, 1-2, 10, 20-21, 25, 37, 41-42, 47, 52, 56-60, 67, 71, 75, 83
Canada (movie theater in Montreal)   16
Coopers & Lybrand   51-53, 67
Cribbage   12
Czechoslovakia   70

D

Davie, Florida   66, 68
drywall   x, 75-77, 83

E

engineering   2, 25, 27, 31, 33, 37, 42-43, 52, 81
Eagle Toys   42
Emory University   70, 81

F

Fairmount Elementary School   16
father-in-law   36, 47-48, 80
Florida   x, 23, 48, 54-58, 61, 63, 66-69, 71-72, 75-77, 80, 84
Folkman, Katie   xi
Fort Lauderdale, Florida   55
FORTRAN   53
France   11, 67

G

General Development   75, 77
gold mining   29
Germany   6, 67

H

Hebrew school   19
Hilton Head, South Carolina   x, 60-61, 65, 71-73, 79-80, 84
Hymie, Uncle (see Kapustin, Hymie)
hockey   7, 11, 17, 35, 42, 69
Hollywood, Florida   55-57, 66, 69, 78
Hudson Bay   28-29
Hungary   70

Hypoluxo, Florida   72

I

IBM 360   53
Iona Avenue (Montreal)   17
Israel   48
Italians   6
Italy   11
ITT   43, 45, 53

J

Jamaica   37
James Bay   28
Jewish General Hospital   36
Johns Manville   41

K

Kapustin, Hymie   ix, 9-11
kosho ryu kempo   69

L

Laurentian Mountains   8, 65
Leventhal Horthwath   66
Levitt Corporation   75-77
Linda (Brenda Bookman's twin sister)   36, 60
London, Ontario   45-46, 70

M

Mackenzie Street (Montreal)   18
magic eye   10
math   15
MBA   51-52, 54, 67, 81
McGill University   21, 24-25, 35, 37
MG TD   22
Miami, Florida   58, 60-61, 66, 72
Montreal, Canada   x, 1-2, 5-8, 10, 13, 15-16, 21-25, 28, 34, 36, 41-43, 59, 69, 76-77, 84
Mount Royal   6

N

Nadolne, Becca   82
        Benjamin   82
        Mollie   82

Nassau   37
New York   2-3, 7, 13, 59
Nortel   34, 39-40
North Bay   28-31
Northern Electric   35, 39, 41, 84
Nova school system   57

O

Ontario, Canada   27-28, 31, 45-46, 81
Ontario Hydro   27, 29-30
Ontario Northline Railroad   29

P

Palm Beach County, Florida   68
Park Avenue, Montreal   6, 16
Philco   10
Poland   6
Polish Arabian   64, 68

R

Rensselaer Polytechnic Institute (RPI)   70, 81

Royal Electric   43, 45

Royal Military Regiment   11

Russia   1-2, 6

RV (recreational vehicle)   70-71

S

Sarasota, Florida   72

Scandinavians   6

Seagram's   67-68, 71

Second World War (see also World War II)   9, 13

Sigma Alpha Mu   24

silver mining   31

T

tai chi   69

Taylor, Ken   52, 67, 71-72

Therieau, Father (Father Therieau)   29

Timmins, Ontario   28-31, 33, 37

Torek, Kimberly   iv

Toronto, Canada   7, 28, 32, 40, 52, 81

Turkey   67

U

United States (and U. S.)   2, 10, 21, 37, 47, 53, 55-60, 66-67, 75, 82
U. S. Gypsum   76
University of Western Ontario   46

V

Vienna, Austria   70

W

Westbury Avenue   20
Westinghouse science program/award   81-82
Winkler, Adrian (Max)   82
Winnipeg, Canada   1-2
World War II (see also Second World War)   9